LEAD WELL
AND
PROSPER

LEAD WELL
AND
PROSPER

15 Successful Strategies for
Becoming a Good Manager

Nick McCormick

Be good PUBLISHING

Downingtown, Pennsylvania

First printing 2007
ISBN-13: 978-0-9779813-3-5
ISBN-10: 0-9779813-3-9
LCCN 2006925375

ATTENTION CORPORATIONS, UNIVERSITIES, COLLEGES, AND PROFESSIONAL ORGANIZATIONS: Quantity discounts are available on bulk purchases of this book for educational, gift purposes, or as premiums for increasing magazine subscriptions or renewals. Special books or book excerpts can also be created to fit specific needs. For information, please contact Be Good Publishing, 102 Patrick Henry Drive, Downingtown, PA 19335; 610-518-2126.

TABLE OF CONTENTS

ACKNOWLEDGMENTS

THANKS VERY MUCH to all of the managers I've had over the years, regardless of your competence. I have tried my best to model myself after the best of you and avoid the poor habits of the worst. In some cases I've succeeded; in others I have not. I continue to work at being a good manager. Along those lines, I would also like to thank the many leadership gurus who have written books on the subject. Your writings have been instrumental in my success.

INTRODUCTION

NOW, MORE THAN ever, management is in a state of crisis. Despite the thousands of books and training materials available to show us the way, we managers can't seem to get it right. Public opinion reflects this. No longer simply the butt of a joke or two, now there's an entire cottage industry built upon ridiculing management—a comic strip, a television show, websites, merchandise, and even part of this book! But don't fret. There is hope. This book and *you* can help.

What you are about to read is a collection of simple, short, and sweet strategies to help managers at any level improve. It is organized in a straightforward, easy-to-follow format. Each chapter starts with a humorous but unfortunately all-too-true explanation of the wrong thing to do. Then the strategy is explained. A list of dos and don'ts that cut right to the chase follows. To make things even easier, the dos and don'ts from all chapters are included in the appendices, so you can quickly reference them in one place. Finally, and most importantly, each chapter closes with actions you can take immediately to implement the strategy.

If after reading this book you choose to do even just a handful of the things recommended on a somewhat consistent basis, you will be well on your way to being a good manager. Do you think you have already achieved *good manager* status? Would you like to verify that? Take a couple of minutes to take the test in Appendix F.

Why just a good manager? Why not a great manager? Well, I'm all for setting one's sights high, but as far as I'm concerned, being a good manager *is* great! It's a very difficult thing to achieve. If it weren't, we wouldn't be in this state. Managers don't become poor on purpose. They don't aspire to mediocrity. In fact, many believe they are doing quite splendidly. They have the best intentions and work very hard. They just don't work on the right things.

Combating the management crisis will occur by training and transforming one manager at a time. You can start by embracing the information in this book. I hope you enjoy what you are about to read, and even more important, I hope you heed what you read and it propels you toward action. Use this book as a reference. Refer to it often. Share your newfound knowledge with others. Lead well and prosper!

CHAPTER 1

Adopt a Serving Attitude

I'D LIKE TO start by introducing you to our fictional cast of characters. The manager's name is Joe Kerr (affectionately referred to by his direct reports as "Joker"). He's been with the company for fourteen years and in his current position for six months. Joe has been managing people in various capacities for more than ten years and currently manages six frontline managers. Wanda B. Goode reports to Joe. She is a frontline leader who manages eight actual doers. Wanda has been a manager for one year and with the company for six. Although Joe and Wanda are fictional characters, the scenes they play out are all too familiar in the "real" world.

Wanda: Joe, the troops are a bit upset about the new directive to enter time into a third system. We already record time in multiple places. It's a demoralizer. Is there anything you can do about it?

Joe: Wanda, you know my hands are tied on this one. Rules are rules. I don't like them any more than you do. I can remember when I first started; we had to enter our time manually on twelve spreadsheets. Believe me, you guys are getting off easy.

Wanda (thinks): Some help he is!

Joe (thinks): Boy, I didn't realize Wanda was such a whiner. I'll have to keep my eye on this one. If she can't keep her staff in line, I'll need to find someone who can.

You are a manager. Your purpose is to direct others to achieve certain goals. One of your prime functions is to assist your team members, ensuring they have the appropriate tools and training, removing obstacles that stand in the way of their success, teaching them, and so forth. The people on your team are critical to your success. You, in turn, must help them to succeed!

Many managers have difficulty grasping this simple concept. They are used to saying, "You all work for me!" Although there is some truth to that, a good manager spends a good deal of time "working for them." If you approach your job with this attitude, you are well ahead of the game.

What do your team members need? Get your butt out of your office and find out! Ask them during one-on-one meetings. Draw it out of them. Once you find out what is needed, do something. Break down the bureaucratic walls; simplify administrative tasks; champion their ideas; help them get to the next level; give them challenging work; ask them to help out as well if necessary.

This doesn't mean you let the team members walk all over you. First, you must help them distinguish between what they want and what they truly need. Second, you must set expectations. They will not always be able to get everything they need, and there will be perfectly valid reasons for that in many cases. You need to explain these reasons to them.

Don't forget to follow up. Even if you are unsuccessful, people need to know that you tried, and that you cared enough to get back to them. If you don't succeed, don't blame it on upper management. I've seen too many lower-level managers get chummy with their staff and the us-against-them—"them" being upper management—mentality sets in. This is not healthy, and in many cases it's not true. The failure is frequently because of an unconvincing argument and/or a lack of persistence.

Do   Adopt a serving attitude toward the team.

- Constantly refer to the team as "my team" or "my group." Rather, use the team name (e.g., the accounts payable team) or simply "our group."
- Blame upper management for your inability to sell.

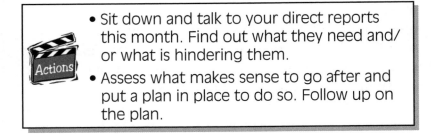

- Sit down and talk to your direct reports this month. Find out what they need and/or what is hindering them.
- Assess what makes sense to go after and put a plan in place to do so. Follow up on the plan.

CHAPTER 2

Teach

Wanda: Joe, can you explain the budgeting process to me again? It's just not clicking for me yet.

Joe (thinks): *Boy, did I get screwed. I'm up to my eyeballs in work, and this one can't write a proposal and doesn't know a P&L from a timesheet! I'll have to remember this when it comes time for her review.*

Joe: I'm kind of busy right now, Wanda. How about I follow up with you in a few days?

(Two weeks pass. Wanda hears nothing from Joe.)

Wanda (thinks): *I guess he's just too busy. Maybe I can get help from somebody else. In the meantime, I'll just do the best I can. I must not be doing too badly. Joe would tell me if that were the case.*

I can't tell you how many times I hear the following from managers looking to hire a new employee: "I need someone with experience who will hit the ground running. I don't have any time for handholding." Guess what? Part of a manager's job is to teach. If you don't spend any time teaching and developing your team members, you're not a good manager. Furthermore, if you're always hiring people with a wealth of experience, you are probably doing them a disservice. Chances are they won't have much of an opportunity to learn anything new in their roles, so they won't have the opportunity to grow. You're also doing a disservice to those eager "up-and-comers" who, with some guidance, can inject life into your organization.

Watch out for "bald tires." Just because someone has experience doesn't mean he or she is good. I know many managers with dozens of years of experience who I'd never take into battle with me. The bottom line is this: When you don't teach, you hurt the team members, the would-be team members, and the organization.

Teaching is quite often a precursor to effective *delegation*. Undoubtedly you have heard that buzzword bandied about. Effective delegation is more than simply barking out orders. If team members are to do good work, they need to know *how* to do the work. It is the manager's job to make sure they know how, sometimes by obtaining formal training for team members but often by informally teaching them.

When do you teach? Essentially you teach all the time. Team members will constantly be observing you. There are also more formal opportunities you should use, such as honest feedback sessions or monthly one-on-one sessions. Pick a topic to discuss at every other meeting. Review a particular skill. Talk about a pertinent magazine article.

Take advantage of the teaching opportunity available with development plans. A development plan is an action plan that identifies the areas in a person's current job that might need development or improvement; it also addresses a person's future goals and aspirations. Activities and actions are listed that will help achieve the goals, as well as dates by which these goals should be reached. Work with team members to create development plans. Find out what they want to be doing in the next couple of years and then help them put together a realistic plan to get there. Suggest and volunteer for activities. Assist with execution of the plans. Review plans in one-on-one meetings periodically.

Getting team members enthused about development plans is not easy. Most find the exercise useless because, although many companies require employees to have them, not much effort is put into creating them. Frequently, no one bothers to execute them. They are nothing more than a checkmark on a manager's to-do list. They often don't get reviewed until it's time to do the next one (usually after an annual employee evaluation is done). Typically, you have to sell one person at a time on the idea. If that person meets with success, share it with the rest of the team. If "Jane" got the promotion ostensibly because of the development plan, that will probably be enough to get others to climb on board. In addition, once people see you are serious about putting in time to teach them and help them succeed, they will warm up to the idea. It can be difficult to overcome years of development plan neglect, but it can be done.

Do 👍
- Take the time to teach and develop your team members.
- Hire those with potential.

Don't 🚫
- Ignore the teaching aspect of being a manager.
- Hire someone just because he or she has experience.

Actions 🎬
- Work with at least one team member to create a development plan. Monitor it during monthly one-on-one sessions.
- Pick a topic each month to share with your team members. If you can't think of one, look at the development plans for ideas. Ask team members for topics that interest them.

CHAPTER 3

Provide Honest and Timely Feedback

(Wanda submits a client proposal to Joe.)

Joe *(thinks): Wow, Wanda really missed the mark on this proposal. She can't seem to get anything right. Now I'm going to have to stay late to fix this thing. Good thing I'm here to clean up these messes.*

Wanda **(thinks):** *Hope Joe liked the proposal. I really worked hard on it. I guess no news is good news.*

(Joe stays two hours late that evening to fix the proposal.)

Joe **(thinks):** *Maybe I should give Wanda some feedback on this. If I only had more time, I would.*

(A few weeks pass and Wanda submits another client proposal to Joe. Not surprisingly, it is similar to the first.)

Joe **(thinks):** *That nitwit did the same thing! Mary really stuck me with a winner here! This is probably the second proposal she's written in her life. Maybe I can work a deal with Pat to transfer her.*

Providing honest and timely feedback on performance is certainly not a new concept. You have heard it many times. So why don't you do it? I'll tell you: You are afraid. You can go on and on about how busy you are but that's not the reason. Giving feedback usually takes a couple of minutes. Being busy may be a factor in a few cases, but more often than not it's just an excuse. I've seen managers do almost anything just to avoid giving someone honest, timely feedback.

It may seem odd someone would fear giving positive feedback, but some fear giving praise when they aren't getting it themselves. They may wonder, "Will it make the team members better than me?"

The fear is much more intense with negative feedback. Being humans, we don't like confrontation. As managers we swear up and down that it's not a problem for us, but it is. We don't like to hurt people's feelings. "What if they get upset? I need to prop them up, not pull them down." Unfortunately, this thinking rewards poor performance, which cheats the company. It also cheats the employees, depriving them of the opportunity to grow and improve.

Don't yell, threaten, or publicly criticize. Instead, take the person aside and respectfully discuss how he or she can improve. Start with a compliment, then offer encouragement and assistance. The important thing is to show you care about the person and demonstrate it is in his or her best interest to improve.

Most will respond positively to this approach and attempt to improve. Those who don't may not be a good fit for the organization. Again, don't ignore the problem or pass it on to an unsuspecting colleague. Good managers fire underperformers. In fact, if you are doing your job properly, it's hard to go more than a few years without firing someone. Even with judicious feedback and active coaching, there is no avoiding a dud every once in a while.

In addition to timely positive feedback, don't forget about rewards. Give the team members meaningful gifts when the situation warrants. Get them something they'll enjoy at a cost commensurate with the accomplishment. It could be anything from movie tickets for a small accomplishment to a weeklong vacation for a large one. Customizing gifts does take considerable time—especially if you don't have an administrative assistant—but it's well worth the effort. If there is little or no money in the budget for recognition, get creative. For instance, you might want to offer paid time off. Most employees appreciate additional time away from the office.

Timely, honest feedback must be given. You owe it to the team members.

Do
- Make giving feedback a priority and do it frequently.
- Couple positive feedback with personal rewards commensurate with the accomplishment.

Don't
- Criticize in public.
- Pass on a problem employee.

Actions
- Compliment someone today.
- Address a performance issue today.

CHAPTER 4

Share Information

Wanda: How was the managers' meeting, Joe?

Joe: Okay, I guess.

Wanda: What did you talk about?

Joe: Nothing special. Just manager stuff. Budgets, goals...that type of thing. Nothing you need to concern yourself with. Frankly, I don't remember much about it. I've been to so many of these things, they kind of all just run together.

Wanda: Do you have any notes I can share with the team?

Joe: Notes? I don't take notes. I don't think any-body does.

Wanda: I don't suppose there are any minutes either?

Joe: Nope, no minutes. This is just a managers' meeting, Wanda. We don't take notes at managers' meetings. We don't have time for that.

Wanda (thinks): *Boy, that seems hypocritical. I'm required to keep meeting minutes, but the managers aren't? And if it's not important, why do they take an entire day away from the office every quarter? They certainly have a lot of perks.*

Joe (thinks): *This youthful exuberance won't last. How long has this one been on the job? Six months? Give her another year. She'll wise up.*

The people you manage are busy. Most of them work hard. They don't always have the time to actively seek out information. In many cases, they don't have access to it. To a large degree, as a manager, you are their sole conduit. So tell them what's going on! Let them know what's happening in your department, in the department next door, in your region, your company, and so forth. Don't keep all the information to yourself. Share it. Don't be afraid to give it up. That's what a good manager does. A bad manager hoards the information, choosing to share only what may benefit him or her.

Don't forget to tell them what you've been doing as well. They really want to know. You probably request a status report from them so you know what they are doing.

They should know what you're doing. I've found a monthly newsletter to be beneficial. It will take about an hour of your time, but it's worth it.

Meet individually with your direct reports at least once a month. Meeting as a group doesn't count. Stopping by their cubicles and asking about Sunday's game doesn't count either. The most common response I get from managers is, "I don't have to set up a separate meeting. I talk to 'my people' every day. They can come to me at any time with issues, ideas, and so forth." Unfortunately, that's not good enough. Employees deserve some private time with their managers. Most are reluctant to call a meeting. They don't want to bother their manager. They are also a bit frightened. A regularly scheduled one-on-one meeting takes care of that. You'll be amazed at the positive effects this will have. Set aside at least a half-hour for each session. Let them vent. Ask them about their careers. Teach them. Listen to them. Ask how you can help them.

Do Share as much as you can, keeping in mind the sensitivity of certain information.

Don't
- Hoard information.
- Cancel one-on-one appointments. They are as important (if not more so) than any other meeting. Calling off these meetings tells the employee that he or she is insignificant.

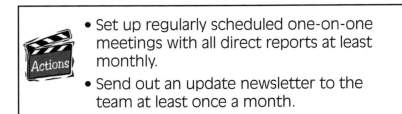

- Set up regularly scheduled one-on-one meetings with all direct reports at least monthly.
- Send out an update newsletter to the team at least once a month.

.

Listen

(Wanda arranges an appointment with her boss, Joe, to pitch an idea.)

Wanda: Joe, I think I have a way to help reduce our inventory costs.

Joe: Okay, let's have it.

Wanda: Well, the overall premise—

(The phone rings. Joe picks up.)

Joe: Joe Kerr speaking. Can I help you? Jack, how are you? How was the golf vacation? Super. Hey, I have someone in my office now. Can I give you a call back in ten minutes? Great. Talk to you soon.

Joe: Go ahead, Wanda. I'm all ears.

Wanda: As I was saying, the premise is to shift the inventory burden from us to our suppliers—

Joe: Speaking of suppliers, did you get that report out to Belgrade Steel yet? They've been all over me.

Wanda: Yes, Joe. I got it out yesterday.

Joe: Great. You know, Wanda, when I ran the operations for Jerco back in 1993, we had an issue similar to what we're having now with Belgrade. I fixed it by increasing communication. I started a weekly conference call with the client. I'd like you to start one up with Belgrade....

Wanda (thinks): *Does this blowhard want to help the business or just talk about his own exploits? I came to discuss my idea, and he wants to chatter about himself and fix a problem I've dealt with already.*

Joe (thinks): *This is kinda fun. I hope this kid is grateful for all the help I give her. No one was around to do it for me when I was up-and-coming.*

Joe: Listen, Wanda, I need to make a call. Did we cover everything?

Wanda: I guess so.

Joe: Great. This was good stuff. Drop by again soon. You know I'll always do what I can to make myself available.

You are not nearly as important as you think you are—so don't act that way. Don't attend more than four hours of meetings in a day. Put down the cell phone and the PDA. Pull your eyes away from your email and spend some time listening to your direct reports. Let them do some of the talking. In American culture we tend to equate leadership with yapping. There is no correlation. Just because you are a manager doesn't mean you have to pipe up all the time. We managers sometimes speak just to hear our own voices. We feel we have to say something at every meeting to prove we're on top of things. Believe me, it's not necessary. Speak when you have something valuable to contribute. Spend the rest of the time listening. Your team members have a lot of good ideas. If they know you're listening, they'll come up with even more. But if they catch you reading mail while they are pitching an idea to you, they will shut down. They won't be back either.

You can help them come up with ideas and solutions to problems by probing. Resist the urge to offer up a solution. Let them figure it out. If you think they need a lifeline, first ask them if they'd like your opinion. If they say yes, then give it to them.

This is another one of those easier-said-than-done items. It takes a conscious effort and practice. There is no shortcut.

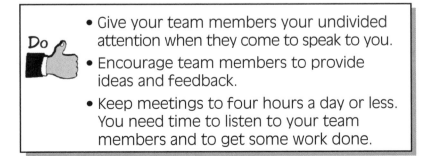

Do
- Give your team members your undivided attention when they come to speak to you.
- Encourage team members to provide ideas and feedback.
- Keep meetings to four hours a day or less. You need time to listen to your team members and to get some work done.

- Bring your laptop to a meeting to read email. How would you feel if your team members did that in one of your staff meetings?

- Answer your phone when a team member is in your office.

- Spend time in your next meeting thinking up what to say to prove you are on top of things. Instead, prepare beforehand and spend most of the time in the meeting listening.

- Speak unless you have something valuable to contribute.

At your next one-on-one meeting, make a concerted effort to listen. Ask an open-ended question or simply request some information—personal or work-related—to kick things off. Maintain eye contact. Don't take notes. Don't think about what question you are going to ask. Just listen. Stay engaged by summarizing what the team member has said. Resist the urge to bring up a related story, one of your ideas, and so forth.

CHAPTER 6

Treat People Like Human Beings

(Wanda gets summoned to Joe's office to explain a major client-impacting issue.)

Joe: What's going on, Wanda? You better tell me you have this under control.

Wanda: Well, Joe, we're working through it. Jason's really the expert, but he's at his grandmother's funeral today, so the rest of the team is chipping in to work it out.

Joe: Wanda, if we don't get this problem fixed in another hour, heads will roll. Get Jason in to fix it.

Wanda: Joe, he's at a funeral.

Joe: I don't care where he is. Get his butt in here to fix the problem!

Although you'd think this would be a given, much too often managers get so caught up in what they are doing (and what they are being told to do), they ignore the fact that they are actually dealing with people. Many of the strategies discussed in this book—listen, teach, share information, and so forth—pertain to this one, but this is so important, it deserves a separate mention.

Everyone is different, but all people have a few things in common. One of them is that they'd like to be treated with respect. Before managers act on something that will impact team members, they should always ask themselves how they would feel if the same thing happened to them. The answer to that question will lead him or her down the correct path.

Dealing with people is not easy. I've heard more than a few managers mention that their jobs are fine except for the people. These managers are probably not in the correct position. Management and people go hand in hand. I'm not saying you have to love all people, but you do need to be able to empathize with them and treat them well.

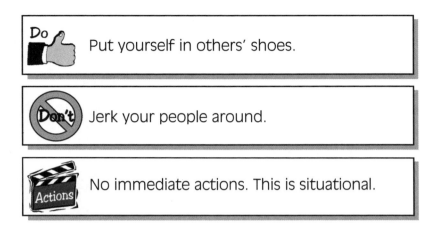

Do Put yourself in others' shoes.

Don't Jerk your people around.

Actions No immediate actions. This is situational.

CHAPTER 7

Set Goals, Plan, and Execute

(Joe has just been asked to spearhead a project crossing multiple organizations. The project originated from recommendations made by a consulting firm.)

Joe *(thinks)*: *We really need to get a jump on this thing. I'll call a meeting for this Friday, then we'll meet weekly until it's done.*

(Joe calls his administrative assistant.)

Joe: Jane, can you set up a meeting for this Friday at 9:00 A.M.? Make sure we have bagels and coffee available.

(One month passes.)

Wanda: Joe, how's your pet project coming along?

Joe: I think we're really making progress.

Wanda: What are the goals for the project?

Joe: Well, this project is fairly complex, so the goals aren't hammered out completely. We'll have to remain flexible and work our way through it. But we're meeting weekly, and that's the important thing. We've had some good dialogue. I think we just need to get to know each other a little better. Then the collaboration will flow.

Wanda: Do you mind if I share your project plan and schedule with the team? I think it would be a great learning experience for them—and me too.

Joe: Project plan? Well, we don't really have time for that. Frankly, we don't even need one; this group has been around the block a few times.

Wanda: When will you wrap things up?

Joe: I'm not really sure. We'll just have to play it by ear. The leadership team is very busy. We don't have much time. I consider it an accomplishment just getting everyone together each week.

Take the time to set goals and write them down. Ensure that they are aligned with the larger goals of the organization, division, or company. If you really want to enjoy and find meaning in your work, make sure your own personal aspirations support them as well. Let everyone know what your goals are and revisit them frequently.

Develop plans to achieve the goals. Gather input from team members. If you have a long list of initiatives, don't make the mistake of biting off more than you can chew. Managers spend months coming up with initiatives and putting together plans. They rarely achieve any of them because they take on too much. Instead choose one to three of the most important goals/initiatives and commit to completing them. Implement them come hell or high water. No excuses. When you finish, pick one or two more. Build on your successes. Review progress frequently with the team. It's great for morale. It shows the people in the organization that things can get done; improvements can be made.

There is no shortcut. You must have a plan and execute it. You certainly can't expect others to follow plans and processes if you don't. "I don't have time" is no reason to nix the planning step. Your team members don't have time either! I'll let you in on a little secret. I don't like to plan and follow processes myself, but I understand the need to do so. It's the path to effectiveness. I also realize that if I expect the team to do it, I certainly need to do it as well. That's the bottom line.

Do 👍
- Set the right example for your group by setting goals. Develop plans to achieve them, then execute them with a vengeance.
- Make deadlines and stick to them.

- Bite off more than you and the team can chew.
- Ignore planning. No one is "above" the need to plan.

Dust off your old list of initiatives. Pick one or two that still apply. Put together a plan and implement it by the due date no matter what.

CHAPTER 8

Learn

(Wanda discusses a book with her peer, Perry.)

Wanda: I just read a great book by Lee Dergood.

Perry: Yeah, I read it too. I really enjoyed it. From what I can remember, it had some good stuff in it…profound even.

Wanda: Ever think of using some of the suggestions?

Perry: Maybe if I had time I would. I'm just so swamped right now. Actually, I don't remember much of it anyway.

(The next day Wanda drops in on her boss, Joe.)

Wanda: I just read that new management book by Lee Dergood.

Joe: Those books are something, aren't they? Those academics ought to see how things work in the real world and spend a day in the moccasins of Joe Kerr!

Joe (thinks): She has time to read a book? I better get her some more work to do.

Wanda: I was thinking of using a suggestion from the book to help us improve our teamwork.

Joe (thinks): Is she kidding? Ahh, the exuberance of youth. It's a shame it's so fleeting.

Joe: Well, before I can give you the go-ahead, I'll need you to do a formal writeup and justification document. There shouldn't be any problem with approval as long as you don't take up any work time to do it.

The fact that you are reading this book indicates that you are willing to learn. Keep it up! As mentioned previously, if you do a majority of the things I suggest with some consistency, you will be a good manager. However, that doesn't mean the learning stops there. I recommend that you continue to read management and leadership books. Most rehash similar concepts, but typically they offer different perspectives. Some will resonate more with you than others. Some will reinforce what you already know. Others will add a new dimension or possibly introduce an entirely new concept.

Unfortunately, all the learning you do is useless unless you put it into practice. So when you read a book that has some good suggestions, implement them with your team. That's the real purpose of the "action" section at the end of each chapter. Don't worry about what others might think or say. "Jane must be nuts. Look what she's doing now!" I've found that in management, as well as in life, if someone laughs at what you are doing, the odds are good you are on the right track.

Of course, management is not the only area you need to learn. You need to learn about your industry, your company, your clients, and your organization, as well as other skills required for you to do your job. I'm amazed at how outsiders typically know more about companies than the managers do. Many managers rarely (if ever) visit their company website. Again, they claim to have no time for that!

Don't rely on your company to give you all the training you need. Certainly you should capitalize as much as you can on whatever it has to offer, but remember, it's your career. If you have a good manager, he or she will probably help, but you need to take control. You need to make sure you are prepared to do the best job you can. You need to get ready for your next position. The more skills you acquire, the more confident you become. The more confident you become, the more secure you feel. You will be much more willing to stick up for what you believe in if you are not scared to death about losing your job. It makes being a good manager a bit easier.

As the saying goes, "If you're not growing, you're dying." Take learning very seriously. I know, you don't have time, right? Baloney again! Make the time. (I have a tip in this area that I'll share with you in the upcoming pages.)

How do you learn? Here are some suggestions:

1. Read trade magazines, books, and so forth. Don't get too carried away with the trade rags. Pick one or two you really like. Subscribing to a half-dozen magazines and newsletters can become overwhelming.
2. Get out of the office and attend some seminars and speeches, meet and talk with some experts. A little networking will help build your confidence as well.
3. Take a class or webinar.
4. Join a user group.

You don't need to do all these things at once. Just start doing something. The bottom line once again is *action*. If you are unsure of where to concentrate your effort, ask someone for help. Start with your boss. If he or she is not willing or capable, ask someone you respect, either inside or outside of your company.

- Take ownership of your career and commit to continual learning.
- Take advantage of what your company has to offer and get whatever else you need on your own. Make the same recommendation to your team members.

Rely on your company or manager to get you where you need to go.

Actions

- Pick a trade magazine that you like and read one article—of any length—every day.
- Attend a seminar, rotary club speech, brown bag lunch, or something similar once every quarter.

CHAPTER 9

Do the Right Thing

Example 1

Joe's administrative assistant: Joe, Kim is on the phone. She'd like you to provide her with some people to help her on a proposal.

Joe (thinks): *No way. I don't get any credit for Kim's revenue. What excuse can I use?*

Joe: I'd really like to help you, Kim, but we're really swamped down here. Maybe next time. Why don't you try Craig?

Example 2

Wanda: Joe, I'd like to give Jerry a 15 percent raise.

Joe: You're kidding, right? This is a lean year. I can barely get 5 percent approved.

Wanda: But, Joe, Jerry's a fabulous employee, and he's way underpaid. He knows it too.

Joe: Rules are rules, Wanda. You know I can't do more than 12 percent, even in boom years.

Wanda: Joe, 5 percent may sound good, but at his low salary, it doesn't amount to much at all. It will take him forever to catch up. I just think if we don't give him a significant bump, he'll walk.

Joe: Sorry, Wanda, I guess we'll just have to take our chances.

Frequently, management incentive programs do not reward altruistic behavior. Words like "collaboration" and "teamwork" get thrown around, but there is precious little of either actually occurring in companies. If you are going to be a good manager, you need to do the right thing—even if it doesn't put an extra jingle in your pocket. Sometimes you and/or your group need to sacrifice for the good of the whole and do what's best for the company.

Exception Processing

There is always exception processing. You are not a robot. You have the ability to make decisions. If your boss doesn't let you make your own decisions, work first at making recommendations. Typically after a few good recommendations, even the most controlling bosses are apt to give you some leeway.

Not everything has a cookie-cutter solution or response. If it did, there would be no need for managers. Rules can and should be broken every once in a while. The problem is that it's always safest to follow the rules, and all too frequently, managers hide behind them. Who can question them if they follow "policy"?

If it makes sense to make an exception, do it. Invest some energy to make it happen.

A word of warning: Exceptions should be just that— exceptions. When exceptions become the rule, you've created an equally destructive problem.

Honesty

Although fairly self-explanatory, this is usually overlooked. Tell the truth to your boss, peers, team members, and everyone else.

Doing the right thing can sometimes impact your career in a negative way. It might require you to buck the system, which will not put you in good favor with your superiors. Even first-rate managers can get fired! So it is important to heed the chapter on learning. It is easier to do what is right if you are not scared to death about losing your job. If you keep your skills up to date and your network active, you will have much more confidence that you can get another job without too much difficulty.

Do 👍
- What's best for the company, not just what's best for the group.
- Invoke common sense. When it makes sense to break the rules, do it.
- Tell the truth.

Don't 🚫
- Work the system.
- Make exceptions the rule.
- Make excuses.

Actions
- Volunteer to help out in an area that will really improve the company, even if it doesn't promise a monetary reward.
- If you are currently dealing with a ridiculous rule, expose it. Break it. Otherwise, this is situational. You'll just have to act when the need arises.

CHAPTER 10

Embrace the Uncomfortable

Joe (thinks): Looks like we won't make our implementation date next month. I should give the
client a heads-up. Boy, will she hit the roof! I
don't want to deal with that now. I'm too busy
anyway. I'll take care of it after I complete my
expense reports.

(A week goes by. Joe has not informed the client of the project delay. In fact, he didn't even bring it up in the weekly status meeting with the client..

Joe *(thinks)***:** *Boy, that was a great client meeting. Joy actually seemed like she was in a great mood. It was a good call on my part not to bring up the project delay right before the weekend. I think I'll just send her an email next week.*

Embracing the uncomfortable, which is really the opposite of procrastination, goes hand in hand with all the others. It's a wonderful rule to set for yourself. We have a tendency to put off the things we don't like to do. Sometimes we never get to them. We actually invent things to do to avoid doing others that are uncomfortable. We gladly complete tasks that are not due for weeks, because we are more comfortable doing them.

Did you ever notice that we're always too busy for things we don't want to do (like telling a team member he or she is not doing his or her job)? Yet we seem to have plenty of time for things we want to do. An old friend calls us at work and we'll shoot the breeze for a half-hour without blinking. Why? We want to talk to our friend. We don't want to talk to our employees. It's not fun.

Unfortunately, when we don't do things that are outside our comfort zone, we don't grow. That's a big problem for many of us. It's not the worst part, though. When we put things off we're not comfortable doing, we hurt others as well. For example, when we don't tell team member Larry he is not pulling his weight, we hurt him because we don't give him the opportunity to improve. We also hurt fellow team members. They know Larry isn't doing the job. They are forced to work harder to pick up the slack for him. They are also keenly aware that Larry makes more money than they do. They see that no one wants to do anything about it. Then at the next team meeting they hear managers babble about how the company pays for performance, and they feel like throwing up. This happens constantly. If managers went outside their comfort zones a little more often, the collective impact would be enormous.

So how do you do it? There's no easy way. You just have to make the commitment and do it. It's what good managers do. You'll be amazed at how great you'll feel when you successfully knock out an uncomfortable task. With each success, it will get easier. Give yourself a little reward when you tackle a particularly uncomfortable task. It will give you a bit more incentive. Then just observe all the ancillary benefits that will arise from it.

- Make a commitment to venture outside your comfort zone.
- Reward yourself when you do.

Put things off. You suffer because you don't grow, and others suffer as well.

Pick a task you've been avoiding for some time. Knock it out tomorrow before 8:30 A.M. Treat yourself to a nice lunch. Repeat!

CHAPTER 11

Clean Up Your Own House First

Joe's boss: We need to find a way to bump up our revenue a few points, Joe. Any ideas?

Joe: I think we're doing just about everything we can, boss. The real problem is the sales group. They just don't know how to sell our products, and they don't want to listen to any of our suggestions. If they did, we'd be flying high. They need new management over there, plain and simple. Bottom line is, until they clean up their act, we're going to be dragging.

Joe's boss: I agree with you. They are brutal. I'll bring it up to Mary again, but I don't think there's much that will come of it. We've been down this path before.

Joe: I was on a call with Sam the other day, and he was so embarrassing in front of the client. He didn't know the difference between a widget and a gadget! Can you believe that?

Joe's boss: I can do you one better. Last Friday...

This strategy really has to do with attitude more than anything else. As a manager, you must maintain a positive attitude. That doesn't mean that you ignore the ugly realities. It also doesn't mean that you have to be happy all the time. (Frankly, people who are happy all the time frighten me!) It does mean that you must work to improve things you can control, and chip away at those you can't without allowing them to be all-consuming.

Don't blame others for problems. As Ghandi said, "Turn the searchlight inward." Look to yourself and to your group. What can you do to improve things? Get your team involved. When you do need assistance from outside your group, make a compelling enough argument so the help is provided. Don't pout if you are turned down. Work on improving your approach for next time.

When you are among your peer managers, don't vent. Your energy is much better spent on finding creative solutions to problems.

Do

- Have a positive attitude.
- Voice concerns constructively. Be prepared to offer solutions—and work them.
- Vent occasionally to your boss but not with peers or team members.

Don't

- Disparage other people or groups within your company.
- Be a whiner. It is, however, okay to voice concerns.
- Vent to peers or team members.

Actions

Pick a problem you have with another group. Pull the team together and try to work out a way to overcome it. Don't let it turn into a blame-fest. Keep the focus on the solution.

CHAPTER 12

Persist

(Wanda has just completed presenting a business case to her boss, Joe, for obtaining training for members of her team.)

Wanda: What do you think, Joe?

Joe: I just don't buy into the benefit, Wanda. Plus, I can't have half the team out for a week during the busy season. You're struggling to get things done as it is.

Wanda (thinks): So much for taking initiative. As usual, I have a chance to really make something happen, and Joe throws up another roadblock. Why do I even bother? I'm finished making suggestions.

Don't give up! Work hard. Follow through. Have patience. It may take some time, but if you adopt the strategies in this book and act on them on a regular basis, you will be a good manager. Don't succumb to the pressure of those who worship the status quo. You can do better—and so can your organization.

A good manager can make a big difference in a company, but it's not easy. Some of your peers may even attempt to undermine you. You may be a threat to them. The ranks of middle management have been decimated in the last few decades. Most managers are scared to death they will lose their jobs. They may not like the fact that you are beginning to stand out from the pack. But stick to the high road. Don't stoop to their level. Remain confident and do your thing. If they choose to come along, fine. If not, you can leave them in your wake.

Take your good ideas—and those of your team—forward. Anticipate objections and overcome them. Hone your presentation. If your ideas get shot down, don't give up. Find a way to make them work. Enlist the help of your team members. Keep at it. Remain positive. You will earn the respect of team members and peers alike.

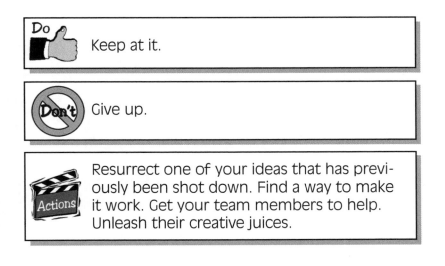

Do Keep at it.

Don't Give up.

Actions Resurrect one of your ideas that has previously been shot down. Find a way to make it work. Get your team members to help. Unleash their creative juices.

CHAPTER 13

Do What You Say You'll Do

Joe's boss: Joe, I'd like you to submit a monthly report on our new client, Sensitivity.

(Four months pass. Joe produced the report for the first two months, but not the third or fourth. Joe's boss calls him into his office.)

Joe's boss: Joe, why didn't you get me that report on Sensitivity this month?

Joe: I wasn't able to get to it last month because I was swamped with the Prioritiville report. You didn't say anything, so I figured you didn't need it anymore.

If you tell someone you are going to do something, do it! This may sound extraordinarily obvious, but just as I don't know very many good managers, I don't know many people (managers or others) who follow this rather basic rule with consistency.

Most managers say they'll do something and then promptly forget about it. Most don't even bother writing the commitment down. Those who do record their obligations often do not add them to their schedules, so they just don't get done. If no one brings up a missed date, they are free and clear. If someone does bring up the dereliction of duty, the managers simply claim they were too busy to get it done. This is devastating to team members who make requests that don't get addressed. It is infuriating to managers and clients as well.

If you can't get something done by the date you said you would, give the requester (boss, client, team member) a heads-up. Don't wait for the day it's due to let them know it won't be done. Inform them with enough time left so some corrective action can be taken if necessary. It is quite possible, for example, that upon learning you can't complete task A on time, your boss will tell you to drop the less important task B to enable you to finish A.

Also, please remember not to overcommit. You can't do it all. Keep in mind, too, that most activities have negotiable due dates, so negotiate!

By now you may have accurately deduced that this is a pet peeve of mine. I actually give a lecture on this topic to all new managers who report to me in our first meeting. I recommend you do the same with your direct reports.

- Write promises and tasks down and schedule time to complete them.
- Learn to say "no."
- Inform your team members of the importance of honoring commitments. Repeat this often.

- Be a weasel and just ignore a request, or stop doing a task prior to getting the requestor's approval to do so. You wouldn't want your team members to pull that on you, so don't do it to others.
- Overcommit.

No immediate actions. This is situational.

CHAPTER 14

Always Follow Up

Wanda: Joe, I'd like to process a bonus request for Sean. He's really done a great job on the ArrowEye project. I'd like to present it to him at the implementation party. The request is in your box.

Joe: Sounds good to me. I assume you have it budgeted?

Wanda: Sure do.

Joe: Great. I'll take care of it shortly.

(One week passes. The bonus request is not approved. Wanda calls Joe.)

Wanda: Joe, any word on that bonus request?

Joe: No, Wanda. I haven't gotten to it yet. It's been really busy. I'll call you after I approve it.

Wanda (thinks): *Why does it always have to be such a struggle? Now I won't be able to give the bonus to Sean at the implementation party. How difficult is it to hit "Y" on a keyboard. How about an update? I don't have time to babysit my requests like this. Problem is, if I don't, they just don't get done.*

(Another week passes and the request is not processed. Wanda has not heard from Joe, so she emails him. One more week passes before Joe finally processes the request, but he neglects to inform Wanda of its completion.)

Always follow up with *everyone* (clients, team members, peers, bosses, potential hires, vendors—*yes* vendors too)! There is *no* excuse. If you claim to be "too busy" to return a call, to look into an item for a team member, and so forth, you are failing (no matter what your management "scorecard" says). Most managers are "too busy" because (1) they are disorganized and/or (2) they are working on the wrong things. Get more organized. Write things down. Work on the right things (the things you don't like to do and those you are embarrassed to admit you are afraid to do) and follow up!

Following up is the decent, courteous thing to do. And it's really not that difficult. Try it. You'll shock people. You'll stand out like a sore thumb and gain instant credibility. Don't dare listen to the nonsense frequently spewed from the time-management nuts. I once attended a class where the instructor advised the class to wait until someone asked for something three times before responding. "That's how you know they really need it," said the instructor. I also had a manager who never read an email message unless it was sent directly to him. In fact, he set up a filter to delete all mail on which he was copied. Where did he learn that trick? A time-management class. Asinine! It's like people are trying to create material for the *Dilbert* comic strip.

Unfortunately, this behavior has become the norm. Customer service has been dumbed down in the last couple of decades. What used to be taken for granted, such as a basic follow-up call, is now considered outstanding. I once got a callback from a rep on a warranty issue. I was so stunned, I actually asked to speak to the manager to tell him how thrilled I was with the service. Think about it. When was the last time you got a response from someone on the first attempt, either at home or in the workplace? It just doesn't happen anymore. Don't fall into this bad habit. As a manager you have many customers, including your staff. Show all of them the respect they deserve and revive this simple act of courtesy. *Follow up.*

Do 👍
- Get organized.
- Follow up.

 Don't
- Make excuses for not following up.
- Rely on your memory.
- Settle for mediocrity.

Record every call that comes in and every email that contains a request. Almost everyone now has access to an electronic to-do list. Use it! If someone makes a verbal request, and you don't have a pen, ask him or her to leave you a voicemail or an email so you don't forget. Spend the last ten minutes of every day responding to these requests.

CHAPTER 15

Plan Your Week

Joe's peer: What's on tap for this week, Joe?

Joe: I'm not sure. I'll have to check my schedule. Jane keeps me fairly well booked with meetings. The little free time I do have gets sucked up by issues. It's kind of frustrating sometimes. My to-do list seems to grow and grow. It's tough to get to it with all the meetings.

Ahhh…. Now we get to the crux of the matter: "How do you expect me to do all these things? I'm *sooo* busy." Let me preface my answer by saying, being a manager is not an easy job. There is a lot to it. There will never be enough time in the day to get everything done. However, to be good, you must get the most important things done. Once you do that, you'll be amazed at how other things fall into place. I'd like to offer a few tips to help make things easier.

Plan your week first thing Monday morning. Review your email, schedule, and to-do list. Determine what you need to accomplish for the week. Write the activities down—preferably in your electronic organizer. How do you determine what is most important? Think about your role. One of your prime functions as a manager is to serve those who get the work done so they can improve their service to the customers. Taking care of the group and helping enhance their performance is important.

But you are not a martyr; you also need to take care of yourself. You and your team members need to learn and grow, so be sure to set aside time each week for yourself and them. You should still have plenty of time left over to dedicate to the other important areas, such as your clients and your boss's litany of administrative tasks.

You'll need to block off time on your schedule for each task. Give yourself extra time for each activity. For instance, if you think it will take you two hours to prepare your budget, allot three. Set aside time to prepare for meetings too. Why? Because one of the main reasons meetings are so unproductive is that the attendees don't come prepared. Don't make that mistake. Some managers have six to eight meetings a day, often scheduled back-to-back, so they arrive late to each one. They aren't prepared, but they rattle off some tired cliche just to make it seem like they know what's going on. They don't take any actions from the meetings either, because they don't have time for actions. They just attend the meetings. They think by attending a meeting they are actually accomplishing something. They are wrong. Don't fall into this trap.

Once your schedule is set, try very hard to honor it. Changes to the schedule should be the exception rather than the rule. For example, if someone calls to schedule a meeting during the time you planned to work on your staff plan, tell them you can't do it at that time. Look to your schedule to see if there is another time that is free. If your week is booked, schedule it for the next week. Limit interruptions as well. If someone drops by your office to chat, do so for a few minutes, but if it looks like it will significantly cut into your prescheduled time (i.e., more than five minutes), ask if you can continue the discussion later. Schedule a meeting, if necessary.

After accomplishing your most important items throughout the day, if you have free time, pick up something from a future day or a lower priority item from your to-do list. You truly will be amazed at what you get accomplished.

Do the same thing the following week. Be sure you review your to-do list from the previous week and check off those items you got done. Ideally, most, if not all, the tasks have been completed. For those activities you didn't finish, ask yourself why you didn't get to them. Carry the incomplete tasks on to the current week's list, then rededicate yourself to improving next week.

I know what some of you are thinking: "This guy just doesn't understand the workload I have. His job must be a joke." Believe me I've been there. I've been the one who worked tons of overtime. I've done it the wrong way, and I've benefited tremendously from doing it this way. You *can* set aside an hour per week to learn a new skill. You *can!* Think about it. What if you were out sick for an entire day? Would the world stop turning? No. It's all a matter of priorities.

"I don't have time" is the most frequently used excuse for incompetence. Some people do, however, have too much on their plates. They are doing multiple jobs. Here's a piece of advice: If you can't get a handle on things from the tips that I've suggested, go to your boss and tell him or her you can't do it all. If it means you lose your job, maybe it's time to move on. Don't try to be a hero. You know the type. They brag about how many jobs they have, how much travel they are doing, how many meetings they are attending, and so forth. Meanwhile their internal and external customers can't get them to return a phone call, let alone get something accomplished. These "heroes" are not helping. They may have the best intentions, but in almost all cases they are performing multiple jobs poorly—despite their Herculean efforts. They are doing a disservice to their team, their organization, their company, and themselves. They and their management need to recognize this and get them some help.

Here are some more time-saving tips:

- If your phone rings off the hook, leave your office and do your work in a conference room.
- Limit reading email to twice a day. Do the bulk of it in the morning. Reserve a half-hour to an hour each morning, and if necessary, come back to it at the end of the day.
- Keep your mailbox clean. Create to-dos out of emails that require further action. Then file the mail away. Delete as

much as you can prior to filing. Keep your inbox down to a manageable level (no more than a page or two). You can't be organized if you have too many items in your inbox.

- Get organized.
- Work on the most important things. Don't forget that the team members in your organization are the ones who make you successful. They are important. Tend to them.
- Use your electronic organizer.
- Set aside time to prepare for meetings.
- Limit interruptions. For instance, turning off the beep notification every time an email arrives is helpful.

- Neglect yourself. You need to learn and grow, just as your team members do.
- Rely on your memory for anything. Write things down.
- Overcommit.
- Try to be a hero or brag about how busy you are. If you can't do a job well, don't do it at all.

Begin planning out your work week. Do it this Sunday night or Monday morning. The first time, it may take you over an hour to complete. Once you do it a couple of times it will take a half-hour or less. It will be the most important half-hour of your week. (See Appendix E for a sample.)

CONCLUSION

THE BEAUTIFUL THING about being a good manager is you don't have to be great. There is so much mediocrity that being "good" will vault you way ahead of the pack. The difficulty is that it's not easy to be good. If it were, everyone would be good. If you make a commitment to act, however, you will succeed.

You won't be able to do everything at once. Put together a reasonable plan (see Appendix D for a sample) and push forward. You will make mistakes. Good managers make mistakes—no one is perfect. But they have the confidence to freely admit to their missteps.

How will you know you are a good manager? Among other things, you'll notice that your team is blowing away its goals and your customers are happy. You'll see team members grow and get promoted. You'll notice that work is starting to actually be fun. You'll have a calm confidence that governs your daily activities. Peers will start to ask you how you do it. Accolades and promotions will follow. It can happen to you. Good luck and *be good!*

APPENDIX A

Do

List of Dos

- Adopt a serving attitude toward the team.
- Take the time to teach and develop your team members.
- Hire those with potential.
- Make giving feedback a priority and do it frequently.
- Couple positive feedback with personal rewards commensurate with the accomplishment.
- Give your team members your undivided attention when they come to speak to you.
- Encourage team members to provide ideas and feedback.
- Keep meetings to four hours a day or less. You need time to listen to your team members and to get some work done.
- Put yourself in others' shoes.
- Set the right example for your group by setting goals. Develop plans to achieve them, then execute them with a vengeance.
- Make deadlines and stick to them.
- Take ownership of your career and commit to continual learning.
- Take advantage of what your company has to offer and get whatever else you need on your own. Make the same recommendation to your team members.

- Do what's best for the company, not just what's best for the group.
- Invoke common sense. When it makes sense to break the rules, do it.
- Tell the truth.
- Make a commitment to venture outside your comfort zone.
- Reward yourself when you do.
- Have a positive attitude.
- Voice concerns constructively. Be prepared to offer solutions—and work them.
- Vent occasionally to your boss but not with peers or team members.
- Keep at it.
- Write promises and tasks down and schedule time to complete them.
- Learn to say "no."
- Inform your team members of the importance of honoring commitments. Repeat this often.
- Follow up.
- Get organized.
- Work on the most important things. Don't forget that the team members in your organization are the ones who make you successful. They are important. Tend to them.
- Use your electronic organizer.
- Set aside time to prepare for meetings.
- Limit interruptions. For instance, turning off the beep notification every time an email arrives is helpful.

APPENDIX B

List of Don'ts

- Constantly refer to the team as "my team" or "my group." Rather, use the team name (e.g., the accounts payable team), or simply "our group."
- Blame upper management for your inability to sell.
- Ignore the teaching aspect of being a manager.
- Hire someone just because he or she has experience.
- Criticize in public.
- Pass on a problem employee.
- Hoard information.
- Cancel one-on-one appointments. They are as important (if not more so) than any other meeting. Calling off these meetings tells the employee that he or she is insignificant.
- Bring your laptop to a meeting to read email. How would you feel if your team members did that in one of your staff meetings?
- Answer your phone when a team member is in your office.
- Spend time in your next meeting thinking up what to say to prove you are on top of things. Instead, prepare beforehand and spend most of the time in the meeting listening.
- Speak unless you have something valuable to contribute.

ur people around.

e off more than you and the team can chew.

gnore planning. No one is "above" the need to plan.

- Rely on your company or manager to get you where you need to go.
- Work the system.
- Make exceptions the rule.
- Make excuses.
- Put things off. You suffer because you don't grow, and others suffer as well.
- Disparage other people or groups within your company.
- Be a whiner. It is, however, okay to voice concerns.
- Vent to peers or team members.
- Give up.
- Be a weasel and just ignore a request, or stop doing a task prior to getting the requestor's approval to do so. You wouldn't want your team members to pull that on you, so don't do it to others.
- Overcommit.
- Make excuses for not following up.
- Settle for mediocrity.
- Neglect yourself. You need to learn and grow, just as your team members do.
- Rely on your memory for anything. Write things down.
- Try to be a hero or brag about how busy you are. If you can't do a job well, don't do it at all.

APPENDIX C

List of Actions

- Sit down and talk to your direct reports this month. Find out what they need and/or what is hindering them.
- Assess what makes sense to go after and put a plan in place to do so. Follow up on the plan.
- Work with at least one team member to create a development plan. Monitor it during monthly one-on-one sessions.
- Pick a topic each month to share with your team members. If you can't think of one, look at the development plans for ideas. Ask team members for topics that interest them.
- Compliment someone today.
- Address a performance issue today.
- Set up regularly scheduled one-on-one meetings with all direct reports at least monthly.
- Send out an update newsletter to the team at least once a month.
- At your next one-on-one meeting, make a concerted effort to listen. Ask an open-ended question or simply request some information—personal or work-related—to kick things off. Maintain eye contact. Don't take notes. Don't think about what question you are going to ask. Just listen. Stay engaged by summarizing what the team member has said. Resist the urge to bring up a related story, one of your ideas, and so forth.

- Dust off your old list of initiatives. Pick one or two that still apply. Put together a plan and implement it by the due date no matter what.

- Pick a trade magazine that you like and read one article—of any length—every day.

- Attend a seminar, rotary club speech, brown bag lunch, or something similar once every quarter.

- Volunteer to help out in an area that will really improve the company, even if it doesn't promise a monetary reward.

- If you are currently dealing with a ridiculous rule, expose it. Break it.

- Pick a task you've been avoiding for some time. Knock it out tomorrow before 8:30 A.M. Treat yourself to a nice lunch. Repeat!

- Pick a problem you have with another group. Pull the team together and try to work out a way to overcome it. Don't let it turn into a blame-fest. Keep the focus on the solution.

- Resurrect one of your ideas that has previously been shot down. Find a way to make it work. Get your team members to help. Unleash their creative juices.

- Record every call that comes in and every email that contains a request. Almost everyone now has access to an electronic to-do list. Use it! If someone makes a verbal request, and you don't have a pen, ask him or her to leave you a voicemail or an email so you don't forget. Spend the last ten minutes of every day responding to these requests.

- Begin planning out your work week. Do it this Sunday night or Monday morning. The first time, it may take you over an hour to complete. Once you do it a couple of times it will take a half-hour or less. It will be the most important half-hour of your week.

APPENDIX D

Action Plan

If you already have a development plan, you can simply append some tasks onto that. Otherwise you can create a simple plan similar to the one below.

First, take a look at all of the actions listed at the end of the chapters. Pick a handful of them and create a plan. (Remember to embrace the uncomfortable when selecting your activities.)

Sample Action Plan

Activity	Due Date
Quarter 1	
Spend a half-hour every week planning out my weekly activities	Jan 7
Take notes at managers' meeting and share with team at team meetings	Feb 4
Pick a new skill to learn	Mar 4
Quarter 2	
Set aside and spend 1 hour/wk to learn the new skill identified in Quarter 1	Apr 1
Start up monthly one-on-ones with direct reports	May 6
Practice listening to direct reports during one-on-ones. Draw out ideas	May 6
Revisit Dos and Don'ts. Make any necessary changes	June 3

Quarter 3

Read a management book (e.g., *The One Minute Manager*)	July 1
Implement suggestion from book	Aug 5
Share learnings from book with team members	Sept 2

Quarter 4

Create project/team/organizational goals for next year. Develop plan/schedule	Dec 16
Revisit Chapters/Dos and Don'ts and Actions. Evaluate performance against them	Dec 30
Create development plan for next year	Dec 30

Some tips follow:

- Keep it fairly simple.
- Make it as measurable as possible. You want to be able to verify that a task has been completed.
- Don't go overboard. Make it attainable. People have a habit of throwing in tons of items in the beginning. Make sure you spread out activities over time.
- Once the plan is complete, make sure you transfer actions into your weekly planning activity. You can even have a recurring generic activity that says "Work item in development plan."

APPENDIX E

Planning Your Week

Identify tasks and objectives to be completed. As they are scheduled in your calendar, mark tasks with an S (for "scheduled"). If there is no room in your schedule to complete certain tasks, mark them with an N (for "not scheduled") so they can be revisited the following week. Scheduling is completed when all tasks are marked with an S or an N.

A sample task list and schedule follow:

Sample Task List

S • Prepare for client meeting.

S • Work on presentation for next week.

S • Set up interviews next week for John's annual review feedback.

S • Review training material.

S • Work client issues.

S • Work action items from last managers' meeting.

S • Complete monthly financial outlook.

N • Work on proposal for XYZ company.

Sample Schedule

	Monday	Tuesday	Wednesday	Thursday	Friday
8:00					
	Weekly planning*	Read email*	Read email*	Read email*	Read email*
9:00	Read email*			Weekly staff meeting *	
	Time reporting*		Weekly project update conference call*		One-on-one meeting*
10:00	Work client issues	Complete monthly financial outlook		Publish mtng minutes*	
11:00				Client meeting	Marketing conf call
12:00					
1:00	Set up interviews for John's review				
		Monthly managers' meeting		Work on next week's presentation	
2:00			Prepare for client meeting		
3:00	Work action items from last managers' meeting				Expense reports*
					Purchasing approvals*
4:00		Review training materials			
5:00					

* Recurring items

Here are some tips for making this work:

- Make sure you have all of your recurring meetings scheduled.
- Give yourself more time than you think you'll need to complete tasks.
- Don't schedule any meetings prior to 9:00 A.M. or after 5:00 P.M. This will leave you extra time to get to unexpected items that may come up.
- If you finish something early, pick off a future item.
- If you fall behind, see if you can make an adjustment to the schedule.
- Share the busy times on your calendar so people will schedule around you.

Before setting your schedule for the following week, review your performance from the prior week. Mark the completed items on your task list with an X. Think about why you didn't get the others done. Carry the unfinished items forward to your current week's task list and repeat the scheduling steps. Reward yourself when you have a good week.

Am I a Good Manager Test

Instructions: Indicate Y for yes and N for no.

1. _____ In the past month, have you done something to make a team member's job easier?

2. _____ Do you share information from all management meetings with your team members?

3. _____ Have you shared with your team members what you've done this past month via a newsletter or team meeting?

4. _____ In the past month have you asked a team member to help you solve a problem?

5. _____ Do you have regularly scheduled one-on-one meetings with your team members? (Water cooler conversations don't count.)

6. _____ In the past week have you given positive feedback to a team member?

7. _____ In the past month have you given constructive criticism to a team member?

8. _____ Do your team members have development plans that are used?

9. ____ Has it been less than a month since you talked with a team member about his or her development plan?

10. ____ Have you presented a learning topic to your team in the last quarter?

11. ____ Have you ever been involved in a meeting with team members where you just listened, without giving advice?

12. ____ Do you ignore all interruptions during meetings (i.e., no answering phones, no reading email, etc.)?

13. ____ Do you keep your phone on vibrate at all times?

14. ____ Have you read a management book in the last six months?

15. ____ In the past six months have you acted on a suggestion you picked up through reading a book or taking a class, seminar, or webinar?

16. ____ Do you have a development plan that you actually use?

17. ____ In the past few weeks have you performed an uncomfortable task (one that was not urgent and not forced upon you)?

18. ____ Have you fired someone for performance problems in the last five years?

19. ____ In the past year have you reworked and resubmitted a recommendation that was previously shot down?

20. ____ The last time you hired a team member from a list of internal candidates, did you follow up with those who did not get the position?

21. _____ Do you respond within twenty-four hours to all those who have called you?

22. _____ Does your group have working plans to achieve a list of goals that are tied to corporate goals?

23. _____ Do you require the same rigor in tracking your own projects that you require from your team members?

24. _____ Do you strictly enforce due dates on internal projects?

25. _____ Do you prioritize your work activities and plan out every week?

26. _____ Do you set aside time at least every other week for your own self-study?

27. _____ Do you set aside time to plan for meetings?

28. _____ Do you review accomplishments from your previous week, reflecting on what was and was not completed?

29. _____ In the past year have you implemented a creative solution to improve or solve a perceived problem with another group?

30. _____ If you can't complete a task by a due date, do you inform the requester/stakeholder prior to the due date to allow for corrective action to be taken?

31. _____ In the past six months have you turned down a task from your manager?

Scoring: Add up the number of Ys.

25–31: You're not just good. You're probably great. Throw out this book or give it to a friend. You don't need it. Just keep doing what you are doing.

20–24: Congratulations, you're a good manager. Continue to work on improving.

10–19: You are doing some good things but could certainly use some significant improvement. Acting on the strategies in this book will benefit you considerably.

9 or less: You have your work cut out for you. Please take some action to improve as soon as possible, or you may want to seriously reevaluate your choice of career paths.

APPENDIX G
Recommended Reading

Blanchard, Kenneth, Ph.D., and Spencer Johnson, M.D. *The One Minute Manager*. New York: Penguin Putnam, 1981.

Carnegie, Dale. *How to win Friends and Influence People: The First—and Still the Best—Book of Its Kind to Lead You to Success*. New York: Simon and Shuster, 1981. (This is a revised edition of the 1936 classic.)

Covey, Stephen R. *The 7 Habits of Highly Effective People*. New York: Simon and Shuster, 1989.

Croce, Pat, with Bill Lyon. *Lead or Get Off the Pot: The 7 Secrets of a Self-Made Leader*. New York: Simon and Shuster, 2004.

Dibachi, Farzad, and Rhonda Dibachi. *Just Add Management: Seven Steps to Creating a Productive Workplace and Motivating Your Employees in Challenging Times*. New York: McGraw-Hill, 2003.

Gerber, Michael E. *The E-Myth Manager: Why Management Doesn't Work and What to Do About It*. New York: HarperCollins, 1998.

Give the Gift of

LEAD WELL AND PROSPER

15 Successful Strategies for Becoming a Good Manager

to Your Friends and Colleagues

CHECK YOUR LEADING BOOKSTORE OR ORDER HERE

❑ **YES**, I want _____ copies of *Lead Well and Prosper* at $14.95 each, plus $2.95 shipping for the first book, and $1.00 for each additional book ordered. (Pennsylvania residents please add 90¢ sales tax per book.) Canadian orders must be accompanied by a postal money order in U.S. funds. Allow 15 days for delivery.

My check or money order for $_____ is enclosed.
Please charge my: ❑ Visa   ❑ MasterCard
                  ❑ Discover ❑ American Express

Name _____

Organization _____

Address _____

City/State/Zip _____

Phone_____Email _____

Card # _____

Exp. Date_____ Signature _____

Please make your check payable and return to:
BE GOOD PUBLISHING
102 Patrick Henry Drive • Downingtown, PA 19335

**Fax your credit card order to: 610-518-2127
or order online at www.BeGoodPublishing.com**